'All those things which we re<sub></sub> illumination, pleasure in the placing of one surprising word beside another, sudden unexpected deepenings, and moments when a line is taken almost, but not quite, to the point of fragmentation—all these are present in Don Coles.'
—Carol Shields

'The verbal stretch that gives Coles's poetry its adventuring thrill is world class ... he has outgrown us and deserves an international readership.' —*Montreal Gazette*

'Don Coles' poem which says so much about the/lost "Forests of the Medieval World" it loses/me in places I've never been.' —Al Purdy, 'On My Workroom Wall'

'Coles is obviously one of the most technically sophisticated poets writing in Canada today, perhaps anywhere in the English-speaking world.' —W.J. Keith

'A poet who has mastered the full range of his voice ... [a poetry] easily elegant in its language, but that at the same time plumbs the depths of human experience.'
—Trillium Book Award jurors Kim Echlin, Andrew Pyper and Michael Redhill

# A Serious Call

# A Serious Call

## DON COLES

The Porcupine's Quill

Library and Archives Canada Cataloguing in Publication

Coles, Don, author
    A serious call / Don Coles.

Poems.
ISBN 978-0-88984-380-6 (pbk)
    I. Title.

PS8555.0439S47 2015        C811'.54        C2015-900867-0

1   2   3   •   17   16   15

Published by The Porcupine's Quill, 68 Main Street, PO Box 160,
Erin, Ontario NOB 1TO. http://porcupinesquill.ca

Readied for the press by Carmine Starnino.

Represented in Canada by Canadian Manda Group.
Trade orders are available from University of Toronto Press.

We acknowledge the support of the Ontario Arts Council and the
Canada Council for the Arts for our publishing program. The financial
support of the Government of Canada through the Canada Book Fund is
also gratefully acknowledged.

I owe the very possibility of this book, as of anything else I've written, to the generosity, forbearance, and, no lesser word will do, love of my mother and my father. She was Alice Brown before becoming Alice Coles, born in Winnipeg and, orphaned at three, brought up by grandparents in the Eastern Townships of Quebec and then by an uncle and aunt in High River, Alberta, whom she loved, read History at Victoria College in Toronto (where she was 'Senior Stick' in 1920) and then taught History for one year at Sackville Ladies' College in the Maritimes before marrying Jack Coles of Woodstock, Ontario, a memorably swift-of-mind and gentle man and one of the U of T's top athletes (tennis and basketball) after he had got back to Canada in 1919 from Arras and other addresses in France.

I hadn't published a thing by the years of their respective deaths which may not have mattered to their feelings about me, but all the same I wish I'd been, as my Dad might have put it, a little quicker off the mark. O well. My love to them both goes on.

# Table of Contents

## poem

my mother said
last night you came
into my room
with your
quiet face from when
you were small

and she said
I was not asleep
I was waiting to see if
it could be long ago

# Two-Hander

To my newborn grandson

There was usually a warning. 'If you're
So set on it', my Gramp would be told, 'go ahead.
But keep in mind he's just a little boy.'
That was Gran. While she was talking
He'd be studying whatever piece of wall
He was nearest to, or adjusting his hat,
The straw one with the black band
Around the bottom of the crown. Then
Out the cottage's back door we'd both go,
Him carrying the two-hander.

It was shaped like a harp. This is
Seventy years later, a long while for
A simile's slow glow to be mounting
Towards a page's, this one's, surface, but
The saw's shape never wavered.
It hung on pegs on the wall in
The entryway, and only came down
Once or twice a summer.

The simile's stronger for the wait.

Its wooden handles were painted crimson,
A dried-blood colour, as I didn't always know.
They were the smoothest things of wood
I've ever held. My hands clench,
Remembering them.

He didn't say much, my Gramp. But
I'd catch him watching me

When we were out there, the two of us
Standing in a pine-tree wood
On a yellowing pine-needle floor, and
Along with the watching there'd sometimes be
An awkwardness in him, something unsure or shy,
Glimpses of all those, which may just have been
What could he do about the years,
Such a jumble when he turned to
Look back—the imbalance between us that
Words wouldn't fix. And meanwhile
My arms would be stretching out towards him
When the saw moved in that direction,
And then they'd be pushed back until they were
Almost behind me, and then further forward again,
And everything repeating.

When the log started to tilt downwards at
Its middle, meaning it was about to break into
Its two new halves, you had to stop right away
And lift the blade up and out. I'd probably have
Taken my T-shirt off by then, and now I'd
Pick it up and throw it over my shoulder.
We'd walk to the stream where, years and years
Ago, he'd stuck a V-shaped length of tin tightly
Among the stream bed's stones. A small saucepan
Was half-hidden among the weeds and he'd fill this
From the water running as from a tap out of
The front of the V-shaped tin. He'd watch
The water settle and clear in his pan and then
Drink all he wanted and rinse the pan out before
Passing it to me. I'd do what I'd watched him do.

All this comes from the two-handed saw which
I'm remembering as much of as I can, only

Because of you, little one, resting among us
In your dream of Eden, and a lot smaller
Than I was then, whose dream never showed
The two of us in a wood together, as we will never be.

# Yearbook

'So brilliant has been her career
we shall doubtless hear of her again',
reads the rubric under a forty-years-ago
school photo showing her standing before
a respectful circle of her peers.
She is a solitary figure with a small smile
and a confident gaze.

She has done so well!

Yet as she watches us from the photo
her gaze is an arrow, it vibrates
somewhere near our hearts.

What is she thinking? Inside the photo,
freshly foreseeing a perhaps-unusual life,
does she wonder at the easy prediction?
Which is not yet a lie, but will become one—
we know this because forty years
have passed and we've forgotten her name.

'Doubtless' was overly optimistic.
Though it was not her word and
it is not her fault, she is only standing
where she was told to stand.

What was it like, instead?

## Il Pleure Dans Mon Coeur

*'Il pleure dans mon coeur*
*comme il pleut sur la ville'*

The lovely, easy lines.
(They are both of those things.)

Walking abroad in his twentieth year
was when he first noticed them,
and tested them aloud
in private moments.

Liking the rhyme of their
*pleure* and *coeur.*
Also the flow of their
*pleut* and *pleure.*

Not guessing how long
they would stay. Nor that they
would be forgotten for years,
and remembered as often.

And it's he who, again now,
is here in his youth and naïveté, lifting
his eyes from the page and
turning his face towards me.

'Ah', I say. He smiles at some
lost thought.

# People I Knew for One Year

Miss Darnley in Grade Two who held me
on her lap once and always walked by herself
smiling in a long coat.
Miss Underhill who gave me a diary
saying I might write something.
Both those women with a lap and a diary
and all their children vanishing
up the grades.

Mr. Stephens who when WWII began
said we should all start a scrapbook.
Bill Houser kept his for the whole war.

Frank Elsom who won a blue sleeveless sweater
with 'Bolo-Bat Champion' on it for hitting
the Bolo-ball on its elastic string more times
than anybody. He was killed on his bike that year
and Lornie Hodgins and I went to the funeral home
after school the next day. Nobody was in the room
except for Frank and he was lying too high up
for us to really see him.

Mr. MacDonald who besides being principal
taught the top grade, VI, for one year,
when I was in it. He said interesting things
every day and I finally, but years too slowly,
drove to what used to be his house
to tell him so.

Mr. Jacques who taught Motor Mechanics
which I took when I could have taken German

instead. He let me off something once
without telling anybody I'd done it.

Miss Boyd who taught the First Grade and so was
the first teacher of my life. She had blond braids
wound about her head like a Rhine maiden
although I didn't know about Rhine maidens
then. In the photograph of everyone lined up
in the schoolyard she's beside Mr. MacDonald.
I'm the one sitting incorrectly with a leg
sticking out.

# Flying

At the Alexandra Palace in London,
a superannuated pile with acres of parking spaces,
hence ideal for bazaars on public holidays,
I once turned in and entered the mouldering place
to pause at a stall run by a cheerful woman with
stacked-up tablesful of baubles of various sorts,
among them a ring which offered itself to me
compellingly, composed as it was of a silver band
with a narrow glassed-over space within which was
a once-fluttery pale-blue butterfly wing. The butterfly
was or had been real, I was told its name and *herkunft*
and forgot these instantly. But I loved the unexpected truth
of the pale-blue wing, that it had flown, and bought the ring
for my then twelve-year-old daughter, who in the first year
of her occasional wearing of that ring broke it and never
mourned it. But I *did*. Mourn it. Actually what I mourned
was the possible lessening, prospective loss, of the longtime
reliance my daughter and I had both surely had on each other,
as shown in numberless transient and unspoken ways—
ways which had never blurred the sightings I'd occasionally get
of indefinite bigger things awaiting her. Those cloudy forms
placated me, a little, for the speeding years. It needs to be
added that she had once warned me about all this. On
an evening when we'd just finished one of our bedtime
readings-aloud of favourite stories, she had called out
to me, quietly, as I began my descent downstairs,
'Some day I will fly away. Like Peter. Like Peter', and I had
allowed the call to enter me in a way she had surely
not intended, which was no particular way at all, really,
it was just a child's voice *en route* to dreaming
and the call was nobody's fault, not hers and
not mine either, at the most it may have been
a kind of intimation from the flown-free
pale-blue wing.

# Two Men

Two men stand on a burning deck
in a photo cut from the front page
of a Toronto newspaper for April 12, 1942.

So, a while ago.

The photo's here because in Grade VI
we all had to start scrapbooks of the war.
It's front-page because these two men's ship,
a German battle-cruiser called *Mainz*,
has just run out of luck. Only hours ago
it was on a record-breaking tear, half
of an England-bound convoy sent bottomwards
in a single week, tanker after freighter after
the same again, and nights with
phosphorescing horizons all round.
But now for the mentioned hours
it's been on its own against six destroyers
and a carrier, *d.h., nichts zu machen.**
Its mostly dead crewmen are lying among
a lot of small fires on the deck behind and
around the two men, although there's
a couple of dozen others splashing
in the Atlantic nearby—their heads are
tiny dark items on the casual, miles-deep
swell. All or most of these will be collected
by the British lifeboat-crews which
you can see just leaving the mother-ship
on their traditional, slightly merciful mission.

The two men standing here could easily
have been collected too. They could then

---

* that is, nothing to be done

have continued living for twice their present ages
and on any number of future nights could have
stood outside their memory-inhabited homes
listening to a child playing the piano, careful
notes from an open window—and musing on
a faraway moon.

That's if, post-photo, they had jumped.
But the cut-line doesn't allow this.
They stay where the photo stops them.
They're going down with their ship.

The photo's been around a long while.
Out of sight for most of that while, but still,
around. So long a while that we can almost
hear their voices.

*'Du ... weg mit Dir. Du darfst nicht hier bleiben.'*
'You ... away with you. You can't stay here.'

*'Hier bin ich aber.'*
'I'm here though.'

(Skip the German original)
'So I see. And if I order you? Into the water?
I'm your Captain, yes?'

(Skip again)
'Yes. And I am your First Officer. And
you know, right now, where I am, all's well.
But to be somewhere else, later, a new ship,
new sea—
I don't think so. Please speak no further.'

Back in 1942 I may have felt that if I would
keep this photo around long enough,

checking it now and then on the chance that,
given time, minds can change, reasons
for living could have offered themselves
to these two ... who knew? But the photo's
always been adamant, and the two men's words,
although contrived, still seem about right.
The water looks closer now, you can hear
its lapping over what the two men
may still be saying, and hear it more insistently
when they stop, when they're quiet.

The newspaper's photo saves them.
Not from the lapping water, it will soon
have had its way with them. But from
every other unknown thing.

A photo got into a boy's eyes
when he was fourteen. Sometimes
two men look out from it across an ocean
and there he still is, using his mother's scissors
to cut something from a newspaper.

# Aschenbach in Toronto

Every Wednesday she came by and
apologized like a schoolgirl
although she was not really late,
smiling and pushing back her long hair—

she had been reading Musil, or
Lessing, or, it could be, Mann, and
there might be some query about
the lecture of the day before, or

she would mention to him that moment
by the sea, on the beach at the Lido,
where the celebrated author is
hallucinating in his deck chair,

and by now they would be
undoing each other and
as their bodies came open
there would be only

a minute or so left
for this, their mouths
pre-empted except for
slight and perfunctory

syllables—
but still that image beckoned,
and still the little subdued slap
of the Adriatic mingled

with the air-conditioning
so that even on the office couch, or
held up against some noticed space
when love was

prompting her, she would see
what *he* had seen,
a kind of god, a stunning boy
on whom the sun paused

turning to look back
from the curling shore, but
it meant nothing,
it was youth

and she was impatient
with anyone who knew
so little. If she
could intercept

that glance from the deck chair,
oh, not to be *seen* by it but
to *become* it—
and at the thought of this,

of pouring forth out of
that cache of mind, collecting
beach and sun and
stunning boy

and returning inside to test these
against the thronged images
*(think of it! always there, always*
*ardent for the light!)*

and teeming, stacked-up rhythms
of that severe, unswerving life,
why, she can hardly wait,
this is why she's here,

this is not Venice and
not exactly an aloof genius
either, but it's the closest
she can get to

things so boundless
she could spend her whole life
investigating them. As for him,
watching

her dress and now the brief pause
and turn to look back towards him
from the door, he's reminded of
something, a motion perhaps,

some gesture, what is it, he wonders,
watching although she is gone,
he leans forward in his chair
by the sea.

# A Tender Tale

Richard Gwyn's fine biography
of Sir John A. Macdonald led to this.

John A. Macdonald, in a second marriage, fathered
a daughter, Mary, who shortly after birth was diagnosed
as hydrocephalic and 'would never be able to stand,
walk, feed or dress herself'. Sad start but, skipping a bit,
what's next are images of perfect love. Extensions
from her first-floor bedrooom are built so that Mary,
in privacy, can look straight down into dinner parties
or straight ahead into dawns; and her father rushes home
from four-hour speeches in the House to tell her how all went.
She lived 66 years and, it may be believed, often happily.
There's more. Years later a second wife will find in the attic
what she describes to the by-then Sir John as
'A box of odd wooden objects' and asks, 'What might these be?'
The knight's eyes fill with tears as he explains that they are
'John A's toys'. 'John A' was the agreed-upon manner
in which he and his first wife had always spoken of a son who
lived for just a year, one August to the next, but for whom
these 'odd wooden objects' were meant to be toys.
In my mind I pick them up, these objects which can hardly
have been played with but which have been in this attic
a very long while, and turn them about for not long at all
in my cautious, undeserving hands. A tear or two
habitually arrives/arrive; a private matter. Is there
more to say? There is, possibly, this—young John A
returns in a September his life never reached, saying,
'These were my toys. I watched them from my crib.'

# The Berlitz Class Goes to the Opera

The Belgian countess offered me her Merc
for the drive from Munich to Vienna
for *Leonore*. Loads better than hitchhiking
with the usual boring lot, she said.
There was a catch, though: she would come too.
The trouble with this was Solveig—which of them
would sit up front? Next thing I knew,
the countess couldn't have the car after all,
her uncle required it that entire weekend.
So in groups of two or three most of us hitched
and everybody got there in time for the matinee,
only to be told there was a dress code which
we didn't meet. Long palaver at the box office,
the house manager and Yves Tran-Ba-Huy
deliberating at length in their mutually opaque
languages, but finally it was agreed that if
we all sat or stood in the same box and didn't
move out of it during either of the intermissions,
we could stay. Thomas Hands, who was Dutch
and wearing a tie, could go out for trays of coffees,
but nobody else.

When I picture what *could* have happened
that year—the countess hangs in, I adopt
Belgian citizenship, am ennobled, every other day
there's a bazaar which the two of us have to
declare open—and on the in-between days,
*what*, I *write*?

Solveig's lecturing, or something, in Uppsala.

# John Brand

Citations from *Nature's Engraver: A Life of Thomas Bewick*,
by Jenny Uglow

Two hundred and fifty years ago he taught
at the Newcastle Grammar School, where he 'did not
have recourse to the strap' (rare
omission for the time), albeit he was large and fair

and 'a jovial man, and as lumbering as his book'
(which was an unhurried look
into *'History and Antiquities of the Town
and County of Newcastle'*). On their way down

to Sunday sermons the faithful would see
him at his singular devotions, sinking to one knee
before the lower shelves of the town's main bookstall
while they slow-marched past him towards (all

this in his own indignant words) the 'terrible time
lost at church'. He stuffed or stowed away
into his amazing pockets, unwrapped,
the books he'd buy, so that those pockets flapped

and even dragged behind him. Two
local engravers printed the bookplates he would glue
into those volumes—bearers of words which, he would say,
might speak for him, or even, perhaps, sing, come Judgement Day.

Here's to you, John Brand.
Will you press my hand,

across the years?

# Moonlight

In a lit-crit piece of this morning's date I find mention of
'a garrulous old cuckold with astrological pretensions',
which causes me to grin off and on until noon, picturing
a kind of be-cloaked Caspar David Friedrich walk-on
gibbering under the moon to a nodding-off fellow-cloakee
while on a remote hilltop his tiny wife lies with her white legs
in the air either side of his happy teenage apprentice.
The moon pours itself over everything as it so often does with
CDF although what's lit up is not always grinworthy: for instance
just seconds ago I glimpsed somebody, I'm guessing Agamemnon,
tossing fitfully in his tent below the famous walls, and now,
what a rush, it's a young Canadian lieutenant during a long
and especially, as he remembered, quiet night in October, 1917,
studying the latest reconfigurations of barbed wire
from his lookout post in a trench 'just south of Arras'.
I've so often wished I had asked him much more
about all that, and right now there's a blurred
couple of seconds which could be my chance,
but in the moonlight and the remembered quiet
I let it go.

# Untitled

A free translation of Goethe's
best-known (untitled) poem

Over all the hills
is silence.
The forest fills
with it. In the immense
quiet only a few
resting birds flutter
briefly. Only wait—soon you
will rest too.

A Serious Call 🙰

# A Serious Call

Dying on a couch in his study after being
shot in a duel, Pushkin was asked if he
wanted to say goodbye to his closest
friends. He looked around at his books
and said, 'Goodbye, friends.'

Grattan's bookshop had a clamorous metallic pull-down
instead of a front door. Crashes at eight in the morning
and six at night.

Six was worst. Well, yes.

This was in Southwark, directly opposite the cathedral
and four minutes' walk from London Bridge. I can be
exact about the minutes because I crossed that bridge
every morning on my way to G's.

If I had started that job a little sooner
I could have been among the thousands of other
bridgecrossers of whom the famous poet wrote that he
'had not thought death had undone so many'.

I could have been one more who was undone.

Nowadays the area's rampant with wine bars
patronized by rich youths who got that way
shifting currencies in nearby highrises,
but in the 1950s it was a seldom-go slum
known as 'the Pool of London' and prowled by
seamen from the multi-flagged ships docked there.

The seamen would come into Grattan's looking
not so much for the novels of current stars
like Graham Greene or Elizabeth Bowen
(one of whom still winks from way up there,
the other not so much) as for English-Swahili
or English-Hindustani dictionaries.

The morning of my first day at Grattan's
I paused by an overloaded shelf and randomly
extracted one of the many 'Everyman' titles
so popular in that pre-paperback era, and stood
leafing this—not for long, I'll guess a minute—

(that random book, unreminiscent of anything
I had grazed with hand or eye before, was titled
*A Serious Call to a Devout and Holy Life,*
and was first published, I noticed, in 1728
by a divine named William Law who
earned his living as tutor to Edward Gibbon,
whose massive, ponderous, tolling rhythms
you're more likely to have run across
than those of his tutor)

—when I noticed that the G's manager,
a man not much older than I was (23, that year,
while he was ... uncombed and unshaven
and, unexpectedly, undegree'd—'unexpectedly'
because in his teens he'd run the table
at the Merchant Taylors' School, normally
an Oxbridge waiting-room like Harrow or Eton),
was looking at me and then was almost comically
not doing that but was looking far away from both of us
and then taking briskly off towards that faraway place—

—as if to distance himself from anything resembling
that look I'd just been honoured by—

which within a few days I realized had been, as looks go,
free of intent, but when first glimpsed had seemed
a reproof for some dire act on my part—
e.g., reading a book on the shop's time.

So much for a look which happened or not
and only a page like this remembers.

What comes next, granted that this poem's
arc has to be brief (since John Rolph, previously
identified here, Kafka-like, only as 'the Manager',
shared his Grattan stage with me for just a half-year,
and the poem knows nothing of before or after)
is this—

We very soon, he and I, though neither said so,
guessed we were likely to get along—and that
this along-getting would be book-based was
an easy one. There were other helpful factors too—
the 'seldom-go' slum was one such, it meant
we had few and undemanding clients, which
simplified our working day wonderfully; added
to which, within a month of my arrival
the world knew that the Grattan chain,
the entire shabby length of it, was rusting out,
its dozen or so links dropping off at a desultory
but accelerating rate; which in all probability
explained the absence of bailiffs brandishing
balance-sheets, eviction-notices, etc, at our
non-existent door.

The crashing one, yes.

And may also explain why, a year and a bit
after my indenture with G's ended, the brand
disappeared altogether, without even a *vale*
in the book-trade journals.

But *during* that indenture? Good to be asked.
What we did, John and I, instead of selling books,
was … we *read* them. Most of the live-long day,
five-and-a-half days a week, we sat reading, reading
shelves of them, entire linear yards of them. With
so few demands on our time, most of our week was spent
lounging, books in hands, in broken-backed but creatively cushioned
chairs in a small room at the rear of the shop with,
for warmth on wintry days, a spool-shaped electric heater
on a low, round, wooden table between us.

Also regularly seen on that table: four booted feet.

And—we were reading only books that we *wanted* to read.
If Grattan's didn't have a desired title (and sometimes
it *did*, thanks to the Everymen), we'd mention that title
to the 'travellers' who regularly called on us from
almost every one of Britain's major publishing houses.
The travellers knew perfectly well that our Southwark clientele
wouldn't be queuing up for these privately picked titles,
but they also knew that the titles looked just as significant
in their order-books as those exotic dictionaries did;
and mint copies signalling our current concerns would, as a rule,
show up by first post the next day.

… I know. *First* post? The *next* day?

What else began happening was this. We'd be
sitting around dragging on our Woodbines-Weights
(those skinny Fifties cigarettes which were typically bought
two or three at a time, the two or three shaken out one by one
onto the tobacconist's counter from a luckily already-opened
pack—tuppence apiece, I find myself remembering—and, yes,
we'd be *reading*.

So, amid the quiet and the smoke—flap of a turned page.
Discreet flare of a match. Realignment of a boot or two
on a low, round table.

Smoke wavering up from a beer-slogan ashtray whenever
                    a stray gust
arrived from the doorless front-of-shop.

And then, *this*. One of us (*there's* an unpersuasive start
to a stanza: forget the 'one' reference, *'this'* was the Manager)
was, one morning, partway through his chosen read
when he found himself among lines of a quality he at once knew
he shouldn't be this face-to-face with, so close to, all by himself.
This feeling apparently had to do with 'waste'—
a waste of the lines, somehow. He'd arrived at the last stanza
of a 'terrific' poem, he said, and he had felt—no, not 'felt'—
he 'knew'—that something wasn't right. Given
the terrificness of the page he was that moment staring at,
he felt an absence, a need—OK, he felt strongly that
something *more*, or *else*, had to be right there, had to be
with or beside him. Something more than just himself, he said,
attentive to the quiet, and time passing.

What this *more* could be, *no idea*, he said. But there had to be
*something*, he said. *Come on*, he said.

And, well, I knew the feeling. You look up from
an especially affecting page, and …

Reader, no need to keep you hanging about.
Once the two of us stopped trying not to notice
what we could do about this, which was (too obvious
to name it but too late not to) that within literature
there exist arrangements of words which call out for,
which *cry* out for, *a reader*, but something *more* as well—
once you got that far, it was easy as pie. When the sentences
keep arriving and the realizations go on stacking up,
the half-guesses that something, which just might be *joy*,
might possibly be waiting at the end of them and might even
last a decently long time—there's this need for
something else.

Or some *one* else.

Yes? We began to circle yes.

I can even remember what the first lines, the first
of so many lines to be read aloud by one of those two
(one of *us* two, sure, but we're so almost out-of-sight
way back there among the years that from where I am now
we look to be a *those*) and listened to by the other one
(roles undecided, who would do what, who would read
and who listen—usually this depended on who was the first
to be prompted by a newly arrived sentence cluster to know
that there was *no way* he was going to move past *this* cluster,
its unexpectedness, without getting some backup)—

and you'll remember, won't you, what's just been said
about those newly arriving, call them inaugural, lines?—

Here are some of them.

*Again the guns disturbed the hour,*
*Roaring their readiness to avenge,*
*As far inland as Stourton Tower,*
*And Camelot, and starlit Stonehenge.*

Brief interjection: Thomas Hardy's lines, although
I remember with a degree of certainty equal to anything
written and sworn to by man or woman, whether Biblical or
Bunyanesque or Camusian, that although they were the starlit
first to find themselves being read aloud in that incongruous
place of the privileged page-turners—

(forgoing six words from a Far Eastern line-drawing, possibly)

—they were not the *only* ones we could have picked.
We could just as easily have broken silence with a paragraph
from that celebrated 1400-page novel (you've read it)
which describes, among the vastnesses of many other things
which it describes, the grand opening ball of a St. Petersburg
social season, and, same chapter, also describes a wolf-hunt
climaxing with, as is usual in such sporting events, a despairing screech;
following which, the hunters plus a bunch of partying teenagers
are shown together in a ramshackle nearby manor house;
all these events showcasing (a term Tolstoy showered after hearing)
a 16-year-old girl called Natasha who is poised before her beckoning life
as stunningly, also as purely, hence riskily, as anyone has been
shown to be in any fiction I know about. For Natasha, the two nights,
grand St. Petersburg ball and follow-up wolf-hunt, are wand-touched,
are inhabited by adoring glances and moonlit whispers, by
sights and sounds we want to believe will charm and protect her
forever, but—and Tolstoy spares us nothing here—life chooses
for her instead a heartless near-seduction, a confused first love,
and eventually an unremarkable lifelong marriage.

Through all of the later stages of her grown-up life
it's as if these just-described events had never happened,
leaving us with, in their place, a reprieved no-screech wolf
hightailing it for the tundra, or a lot of thrilled hours
waiting to be enacted, or not, in a ramshackle manor house.
In the latter scene it's Natasha & friends in what are now
music-stilled rooms with fingers held up to lips
semaphoring 'hush, do hush' or 'forget, forget all this',
or 'nothing, nothing has happened here'—which we can
think about or ignore just as we choose. But we can re-enter
ballroom or manor house every fifth, say, or ninth or even
tenth year, and the half-forgotten, half-remembered
16-year-olds will, on our arrival, turn glowing faces
towards us as no others have done since the last time
we read their story—or at least, going for exactness here,
no others since those who will always, out of their unrivalled
nearness, speak to us from 'As You Like It' or 'The Tempest'
or anything else further along on that same shelf.

Among the many potential readings-aloud which John and I
never found the right day for—they're flooding towards me
now—I can see that frozen river in *Anna Karenina*
upon which Anna's niece Kitty is incising her delicate patterns
while the love-struck Levin hurries towards rink and gliding girl
and, slowing his approach as he nears her, despairs of ever
speaking to her again about anything, anything—surely
never of the marriage proposal which is the only reason
he has come to Moscow. Because what's the use?
All the skaters on this shining ice-field are in love with her,
aren't they? How could they not be? And how can he
bear this? These joyous cries speeding past him towards
the certified happiness of their waiting lives—
he should never have allowed himself to see and hear
them like this, never have come so close, never have
hastened through the snow as he has done. So much

whiteness, such longing. All that's left for him now
is to go back to Pocrovskoye and grow old as fast as he can
and die.

Well, he doesn't, but he thought about it.

That's by way of acknowledging that there were
'great books' which we failed to find among
our Everymen and didn't ask our travellers
to rummage after. And why not? Because
we all know everything that we need to know
concerning wolf-hunts and ramshackle manors
and walks towards rivers that become rinks, and if we've
mislaid a detail or two we can pluck their stories from
known niches on our shelves whenever we want to,
can't we? Yes we can. Whereas most people don't,
or not half as securely, know those stanzas within which
Thomas Hardy has invoked the long resonances of those
great grey stones out there somewhere between
the ocean and history.

Well, it's so, most people don't. Though now's
their chance.

Cut to the c. From now on what you'll find here will be
lines lifted out of the same riches-drenched air as that which
you've just been noticing on your skin at Stonehenge. So
buckle up.

Though I confess to a continuing reluctance to abandon
that circle of uncomprehended stone. I've read and re-read
Hardy's poem, which is called 'Channel Firing'—and you may
want to know that in what was then called The Great War,

people living in England's southeastern counties, Kent, Sussex,
at times even as far as London, could hear the guns from France
all day and half the night. And I know those gun-stutterings
pretty well (no, I wasn't there, but I *read*)—and I *do*, truly,
get the point of that mostly unfamiliar tower name, 'Stourton'—
the point being (it's not hard to work this out) that Hardy needed
a word, needed a sound, that started with 'st', he needed it
to set things up for the *next* two 'st' sounds that would importantly
follow, that *had* to follow—especially the killer place name at the end.
And I'm just as moved as he wanted us all to be at poem-finish,
all of us recognizing the power that the poem has as it closes in on
those great, famed, lying-in-waiting
huge stones under still stars.

And I can guess at—and envy!—the week-long, no,
surely month-long celebration that the poet must, privily,
not a word to anyone else, have allowed himself when
'starlit' locked into its perfection-slot in that last line.

Enough poetics; time for sublimities. Beginning with,
what could be more natural, a few out-takes from
the finest novel in the language, a book named for
an imaginary middle-of-England market town,
a 'middle march', and one from which, for a series
of mornings extending into afternoons, the Manager and I,
prompted by passages, would either read aloud or
listen to the other's reading-aloud of lines which
lifted unhurriedly into the nearby air and seemed to say,
*pay us all the attention you've got, we're worth it*—
and I, as usual agreeing with anything italicized,
found sentence after sentence and page after page
in this two-volume work possessed of a more persuasive
(convincing, continuous) rightness than almost anything
I'd ever read.

OK, than *anything*.

In the first of these a wisdom-seeking 19-year-old named
Dorothea is trying to console a recently married, pretty,
shallow woman named Rosamund who will survive
this tense and tearful scene and will persevere with her
half-deliberate and ultimately successful program
of obliterating her idealistic husband's dreams.

It's a long scene in which 'the emotion had wrought itself
more and more into [Dorothea's] utterance, till the tones
might have gone to one's very marrow, like a low cry from
some suffering creature in the darkness.' A page later
that scene ends in 'an earnest, quiet good-by without kiss …
there had been between them too much serious emotion
for them to use the signs of it superficially.'

There are hundreds of swift, unemphatic passages of that
same rarely rivalled quality in the 800-odd pages which
the Manager and I spent, in those days, our time among.
Here are the very last lines of Dorothea's long story
(lines which have been, it's my certainty, meaningful
in unusually personal ways to unusually many readers):
'Her full nature … spent itself in channels which had no great name
on the earth. But the effect of her being on those around her
was incalculably diffusive: for the growing good of the world
is partly dependent on unhistoric acts; and that things are
not so ill with you and me as they might have been,
is half owing to the number who lived faithfully a hidden life,
and rest in unvisited tombs.'

A number of readers, having read the above, may now be thinking quite intently, for a few minutes, of someone privately known to or loved by them. You (it's not an afterthought) may be one of them. Mary Ann Evans, a.k.a. George Eliot, is surely describing here a person she loves. Her description, though it be of an un-named person, one she keeps secret even from this intimately peopled story, allows *you* to bring to mind, possibly from very far off, someone you know or, just as possibly, love. As it has several times done for me. If this is what is happening, then we are deepening our knowledge of a loved person through a description of her written long before she was born. Or of him ... before he. This is uncanny and beautiful. I know of no writer who touched such chords more often and more unerringly—less erringly?—than this writer did, and, through the finely meshed (centuries'-old medieval weavings come to mind) passion of her pages, still does.

Next? The Manager and I awarded, sporadically, from the comfort of our fraying unsprung loungers, *Pour la Mérite* badges to this or that writer. John, whose French easily surpassed mine thanks to his wartime service in the British army's intelligence section in Alexandria and Cairo (towns where that language, until El Alamein, was more in demand than English) thought *Madame Bovary* the *mot-juste*-est novel ever. I didn't disagree but have never much enjoyed experiencing it— so much hurt and bewilderment, and not a merciful syllable in sight. I did, however, learn that F's *Collected Letters* were the finest writer's letters I had ever read, and years later, reading them along with my students, I felt so still. This now is from one of those letters, written from his mother's home in Rouen to his lover, Louise Colet, in Paris. 'It is a delicious thing to write, whether well or badly—to be no longer yourself but to move in an entire universe of your own making'.

The letter continues with a description of his feelings during
a day's work on Emma Bovary's afternoon ride in the forest
with her lover. 'Today, man and woman, lover and beloved,
I rode in a forest on an autumn afternoon under the yellow leaves,
and I was also the horse, the leaves, the wind, the words
my people spoke, even the red sun that made them half-shut
their love-drowned eyes.'

It's almost as good in French.

Take a breath.

And having taken it, the Manager would probably wish to
add, from among other cherished sounds now gone quiet in
his library, a few throwaways. *'Ce qui est beau est morale'*,
*'Ne répondre que par des belles oeuvres'*, 'The less you feel
a thing, the more capable you are of expressing it as it is',
and, from 'Un Coeur Simple', a story so tender in its depiction
of a young peasant girl grown old through pitiless decades of
domestic abuse that its author's designation as chief cynic-of-letters
in his homeland is, *mon Dieu*, macabre.

OK, John? Anyone missing here? Ah, bloody yes, how could we...?
Missing until this stanza was the writer everyone was falling for
that year, his trenchcoat, his cigarettes, his women,
his wall-to-lean-against, and that famously laconic opening,
*'Aujourd'hui, maman est morte. Ou c'était peut-être hier ...'*
Plus several thousand more lines that are so vibrant
they'll never go away. 'It is not humiliating to be unhappy',
'Absurdity is king, but love saves us from it', and 'I do at least
know this, that the work of a man's life is nothing other than
a meandering quest to find again, through the detours of art,
the two or three simple and great images upon which his heart,
at the very first, opened up'.

Pretty good.

He was also, and I tend to feel fine about closing his time
in this poem thusly, capable of this: 'I would gladly surrender
ten hours of conversation with Albert Einstein for a first rendezvous
with a pretty chorus-girl—though I admit that at the tenth rendezvous
I'd be longing for Einstein or a serious book'.

The 'Great Books' people in Chicago were, that Grattan year,
in the process of releasing their early required-reading lists,
and some of their trumpeted choices made it past our crashing
drawbridge as well. But we also had numbers of apparently
unGreats on our list, and among the who-cares greatest of these
were, for us two, these couple of titles. For me, Scott Fitzgerald's
*Tender Is the Night*. Less fine, this was, for my co-conspirator,
who competitively praised *Under the Volcano*, from which
a few words will be along soon. *Tender* has a final scene
which shows Dick Diver (whom we first meet on a Cannes beach
moving 'gravely about with a rake') now in the last pages
'blessing' that same Cannes beach from a high-up terrace.
'As he stood up, he swayed a little; he did not feel well anymore—
his blood raced slow'; and readers may find themselves
thinking back to the much younger and quicker-blooded
Rosemary, standing very close to him 300 pages earlier,
who lived then and can, for us, live again and again,
as often as we pick up the book, 'for a moment ... in
the bright blue worlds of his eyes, eagerly and confidently'.

'Eagerly'—is there any writer who has signed up under this word
as defiantly as this one kept on doing?

Here's a quick side-by-side with no losers, both with identical rhythms and a shared taste in imagery, passages from *Tender Is the Night* and *Under the Volcano*. The first is Fitzgerald's opening paragraph; the second, almost as audibly slapping its thighs to get going, is from Lowry's page 2, para. 1.

'On the pleasant shore of the French Riviera, about half way between Marseilles and the Italian border, stands a large, proud, rose-colored hotel. Deferential palms cool its flushed façade, and before it stretches a short dazzling beach ... but when this story begins only the cupolas of a dozen old villas rotted like water lilies among the massed pines between Gausse's Hôtel des Étrangers and Cannes, five miles away.'

'Slightly to the right and below them, below the gigantic red evening, whose reflection bled away in the deserted swimming pools scattered everywhere like so many mirages, lay the peace and sweetness of the town. It seemed peaceful enough from where they were sitting. Only if one listened intently ...'

Well, Lowry has the best verb-clause—'bled away'—by a country kilometre. Consider what you lose if you substitute 'shimmered off' or 'was mirrored'. 'Sweetness' is unexpectedly likeable too. So Lowry wins?

John ... ? Too late.

I'll still take Fitzgerald's story anytime.

And now it's back to *les grands livres*, and a translation. 'A word read in a book in our childhood always contains within its syllables the swift wind and the brilliant sun of the morning when we first read it.' How vital is 'the *swift* wind' here? Try the sentence without it.

47

And elsewhere in his twelve volumes, same theme,
Proust writes that if he should, grown up, find a once-loved
childhood book, 'I would never look at it; I should be
too much afraid that, little by little, my impressions of today
would insert themselves in it and blot out the earlier ones,
I should be fearful that when I asked it to evoke again
the child who carefully spelt out its title in his little room
at Combray, that child would no longer respond to my appeal
and would forever be buried in oblivion.'

And now, the same piercingly original sensibility (admitting,
though, even as you turn the page, that this writer's next
dozen pages might well be as über-minusculely focused,
hence as enthusiasm-annihilating, as any dozen pages
you've ever stared about the room hoping for rescue from),
this: the teenage Marcel is travelling through the countryside
with his aunt in a horse-drawn carriage, and here are his thoughts.
'I watched the trees gradually withdraw, waving their
despairing arms, seeming to say to me, "What you fail
to learn from us today, you will never know. If you allow us
to drop back into the hollow of this road from which we
sought to raise ourselves up to you, a whole part of yourself
which we were bringing to you will fall forever into the abyss".'

Does it for me, anyhow. I think that no living-or-dead writer
can awaken within us such a deep longing for a lost scene
or sound which we neither knew we had seen or heard, nor,
it follows, knew we had lost.

I conclude this quotation-littered section with phrases
from a man who bestrode (yes, old-type verb)
the literary scene in Britain at war's end in 1945,
and held that position for three further decades.
This was Cyril Connolly, who founded and edited
the monthly magazine *Horizon*, the only literary
periodical allowed enough paper for a serious print-run
during the paper-rationed wartime years. This gave
Connolly a head start on the competition which
for the mentioned period of time nobody could haul back.
When I arrived in the neighbourhood, *Horizon* was no more,
but by then Connolly had a new bully-pulpit as No. 1 bookperson
for *The Sunday Times*, and was mightily influencing people
such as, to point to only two of them, the Grattanfolk
so omnipresent in your right-now pages. Aside from his journalism,
Connolly also published, using the pseudonym 'Palinurus',
a 'word-cycle' entitled *The Unquiet Grave*, consisting of,
for the most part, confident ruminations on life and letters.
I could go into that pseudonym with, if anybody asked,
a coxcombical amplitude, but this would mean re-drowning
and then re-butchering the corpse of Palinurus, who had been,
prior to enduring all kinds of really hard-luck events, Aeneas's
steersman on the latter's galley-way from Troy via Carthage
to Rome; so, no. What I valued most and still admire about
Connolly was and is not so much his elegiac prose,
also not his laments for his kicked-about pet lemurs,
and not much, although some, for the 'unhappy and sullen' girl
he pessimistically trails after in Soho one Sunday 'cursing
the upbringing which after all these years has left me
unable to address a stranger' (a disability which,
I'll mutter briefly here, you don't have to have attended
Eton, as Connolly did, to know something about). But I do
altogether respect not a few of his *obiter dicta* along the lines
of 'Let us consider if there is any living writer whose silence
we would consider a literary disaster.' Also two other,

not unrelated, lines, both of which I might be even *more*
head-furiously-nodding-in-agreement-with—'The more books
we read, the sooner we perceive that the true function
of a writer is to produce a masterpiece', and 'Writers
engaged in any literary activity which is not their attempt
at a masterpiece are their own dupes'.

Those are putting-it-on-the-line statements such as
I haven't read the like of since Connolly fell off all the pages.
He never did manage that masterpiece and his one novel,
*The Rock Pool*, is derivative and, as befits such borrowings, brief;
and there's a list-prone and much-quoted-from text entitled
*Enemies of Promise*. But for me it will always be the mentioned
*Grave* which I'll remember most fondly. I gave away
my greatly marked-up first and then also second and maybe
even third edition of this very thin book, probably to persons
whose taste I was overvaluing, copied its cadences for a decade
or two, and then, I hope, moved on, though there are probably
fingerprints on this or a nearby page which Connolly
would wince or chuckle over.

And I now remember seeing, decades ago, a very small-print
item low down on the front page of *The Times* recording
his divorce on the grounds of his wife's adultery with
his publisher—which, remembering as I did his frequently
recorded and doting domestic enrapturements, caused me
to leave page 2 of that *Times* unbothered for a bit.

In the wintertime of that year there was also, and this
encounter too I owe to 'the Manager', a tiny used-book shop
just round the corner from Grattan's owned by a luckily
equally tiny (and hugely well-read) man named John Uglow,
who was, just then, in the webs of bankruptcy, and who,

convinced that his entire stock was going to be trucked away
to some 'unspeakable place' where it would be sold
neither by title nor by author's name but, 'pornographically',
by weight, pressed both John and, in hardly at all less urgent fashion,
me, during several shared pub lunches, to carry off with us
as many *gratis* books as we could stuff into the very large and strong
brown-paper bags which he provided. And which, protesting the while,
but at least paying for the lunches, we did.

Many a title still tilting on my shelves came to me in this manner,
among them a half-shelf of early-times mystics, one of these
another Everyman to go along with that first-morning-at-Grattan's
title—this belated one called *The Signature of All Things* and
written by a Bavarian shoemaker, Jacob Boehme, whose name
you may find being praised and also loved not only in
the far-above-mentioned *Serious Call* by William Law, but also,
of all things, by me.

I approach the last page.

In addition to the 'Manager' title of which I have made
extravagant use in this memoir, and self-evidently closer to
his heart, John Rolph had, not long before my arrival in
Southwark, founded a small publishing-house, poetry only,
which he named the Scorpion Press. By that time he had
published two collections, one a first appearance by
the Australian-turned-Cornishman Peter Porter, who later
took English citizenship and made it up to
fifth-or-sixth-best-regarded poet in the land; the other
was also a first book, this one by Bernard Kops,
who in the months this narrative is now passing through,
sold, or attempted to sell, his own book and possibly
PP's as well, from a barrow in the Charing X Road.

He must have been, out there in the foot-stamping weather,
the only bookseller operating out of a bleaker venue than,
to the passerby along Borough High Street in Southwark
in the mid-1950s winter, Grattan's must have looked to be.

Later John Rolph was to move, with his wife and two sons,
to the North Sea town of Lowestoft, where he opened
an antiquarian-book business and, near the end of his life,
developed an interest which involved him in devoting, as he
wrote to me to explain, a few minutes' calm and untroubled
thought at the start of each day directed towards
one or another of a small number of friends, among whom,
me. Such a thought was not a prayer, he explained;
and, clearly not content with this, added that he himself was
'never a pray-er'. That note ended with him
expressing the hope that one day someone might find
a name for what this non-praying, prayer-less, thought
*was.*

My most recent and, obviously, last note to him, sent
two years and two months ago, was answered by
his widow. I'd written to ask how, with regard to the title
which he had not, so far, found for that early-morning
thought concerning chosen friends, he would feel about
'a call'.

It wouldn't have to be serious, that call, I'd said.
Or it could be. Whatever he decided (was what I wrote)
I'd probably get to know about it, one way or another.

# Notes

p. 16, 'Il Pleure Dans Mon Coeur', two lines are quoted from Paul Verlaine's poem of the same title.

p. 26, 'Tender Tale', lines are quoted from *John A: The Man Who Made Us, The Life and Times of John A. Macdonald*, by Richard Gwyn.

p. 28, 'John Brand', lines are quoted from *Nature's Engraver: A Life of Thomas Bewick*, by Jenny Uglow.

p. 33, 'A Serious Call', line is quoted from 'The Wasteland' by T.S. Eliot.

p. 39, 'A Serious Call', lines are quoted from 'Channel Firing', by Thomas Hardy.

p. 43, 'A Serious Call', lines are quoted from *Middlemarch*, by George Eliot.

pp. 44–45, 'A Serious Call', lines are quoted from Flaubert's *Collected Letters, Madame Bovary* (Gustave Flaubert's original and Lowell Bair's translation into English, Norton Critical Edition) and 'Un Coeur Simple'.

pp. 44–46, 'A Serious Call', lines are quoted from works by Albert Camus.

p. 46, 'A Serious Call', lines are quoted from *Tender Is the Night*, by F. Scott Fitzgerald.

p. 47, 'A Serious Call', lines are quoted from *Under the Volcano*, by Malcolm Lowry.

pp. 47–48, 'A Serious Call', lines are quoted from C.K. Scott Moncrieff's translation of *Remembrance of Things Past*, by Marcel Proust.

pp. 49–50, 'A Serious Call', lines are quoted from *Unquiet Grave*, by Cyril Connolly.

# Acknowledgements

'Two-Hander' appeared in *PN Review 202* (U.K.), edited by Michael Schmidt, November/December 2011.

'Aschenbach in Toronto' appeared (with a slightly different title) in *The London Magazine*, (U.K.), edited by Alan Ross, October/November 1992, and in *Quarry*, edited by Steven Heighton, Vol. 42, No. 2, 1993.

'Moonlight' appeared in *The Malahat Review*, edited by John Barton, Autumn 2013.

'John Brand' appeared in *Literary Review of Canada*, Vol. 23, No. 1, January/February 2015.

'*Il Pleure Dans Mon Coeur*' appeared in *The Walrus*, February 2015.

# Thanks

I want to record my warm appreciation of the multi-mini-conferences my editor, Carmine Starnino, and I have had during this book's preparation. And to Chandra Wohleber, who can proofread anything I do from now on.

And to Tim and Elke for, year after year, the best-looking pages.

# A Note About the Type

The text face is Junius, named for Franciscus Junius, a pioneer of Germanic philology who was born at Heidelberg in 1591. The letterforms were digitized in the early 1990s from the Pica Saxon used to print Georges Hickes' *Thesaurus* (Oxford: Sheldonian Theatre, 1703–1705). Junius is primarily designed for use by medievalists, and is readily available for download from the English Department at the University of Virginia. In this case the face seems singularly appropriate to a collection of poems in which an antiquarian bookshop in Southwark figures prominently.